Let's Practice Sight Words

Ages 4+

Contents

Sight Words: **a, and, can, come, day, do, down, find, for, go**..........2–11

Sight Words: **he, her, him, I, in, is, it, look, make, my**....................12–21

Sight Words: **not, said, see, she, the, there, to, up, we, you**........22–31

I Know Sight Words...32

Brighter Child®
Carson-Dellosa Publishing LLC
PO Box 35665
Greensboro, NC 27425 USA

© 2018 Carson-Dellosa Publishing LLC. Except as permitted under the United States Copyright Act, no part of this publication may be reproduced, stored, or distributed in any form or by any means (mechanically, electronically, recording, etc.) without the prior written consent of Carson-Dellosa Publishing LLC. Brighter Child® is an imprint of Carson-Dellosa Publishing LLC.

Printed in the USA • All rights reserved.
02-281181151

ISBN 978-1-4838-4605-7

Let's Practice Sight Words

Sight Word: a

a

Circle **a**. Draw a line to see if you won tic-tac-toe!

a	an	an
and	a	is
and	as	a

Color the water blue.

Sight Word: and

and

Write the missing letters to spell **and**.

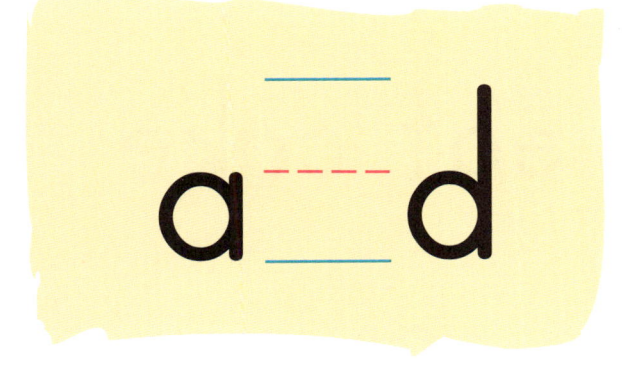

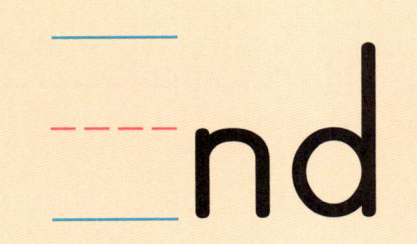

a _ d

_ _ nd

an _

a _ d

Circle the animals that go together.

Let's Practice Sight Words

Sight Word: can

can

Write **can** to complete each sentence.

Jo _____ eat cake.

I _____ run fast.

Jay _____ play ball.

Draw an **X** on the picture that does not belong.

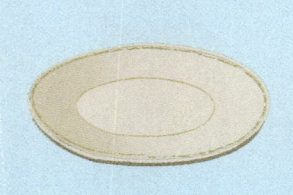

Let's Practice Sight Words

Sight Word: come

come

Color the lemons with **come**.

come   can   came

come   cake   come

Circle the fruit whose name rhymes with **beach**.

apple   peach   pear   orange

Let's Practice Sight Words

Sight Word: day

day

Unscramble the letters to spell **day**.

ayd

dya

yad

ayd

Trace the path with a crayon three times. Use a different color each time.

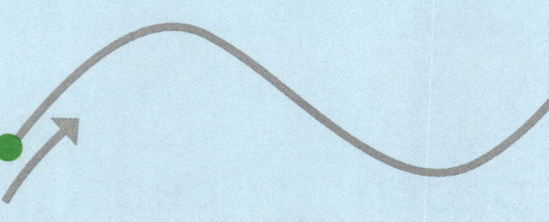

Sight Word: do

do

Circle **do**. Draw a line to see if you won tic-tac-toe!

odd	do	come
does	do	dot
day	do	can

Color the picture whose name begins with the sound you hear at the beginning of **duck**.

Let's Practice Sight Words

Sight Word: down

down

Unscramble the letters to spell **down**.

dwon

nowd

ownd

wdno

Color the shell with **w**.

m   v   w

8

Let's Practice Sight Words

Sight Word: find

find

Write the missing letters to spell **find**.

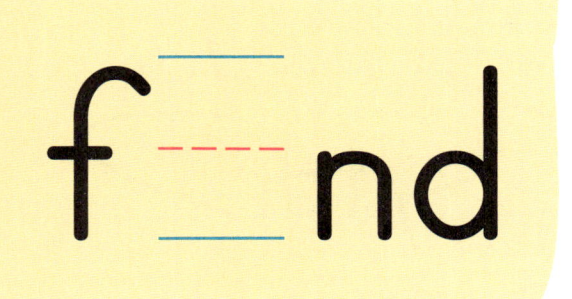

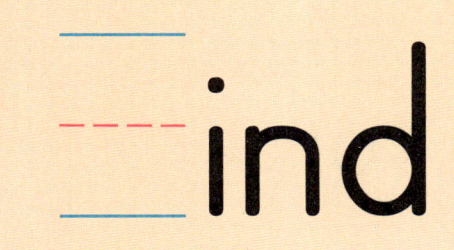

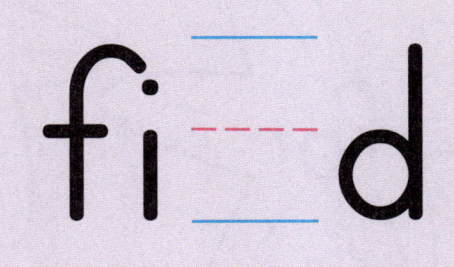

f _ _ nd

_ _ ind

fin _ _

fi _ _ d

Trace the path with a crayon three times. Use a different color each time.

Let's Practice Sight Words

Sight Word: for

for

Color each starfish with **for**.

for — far — for

for — or — for

Read the words. Find two pairs of opposites.

day — bottom — night — top

Sight Word: go

go

Write **go** to complete each sentence.

My wagon can _____.

He can _____ to work.

She can _____ to school.

Circle the letters.

Let's Practice Sight Words

Sight Word: he

he

Circle the notes with **he**.

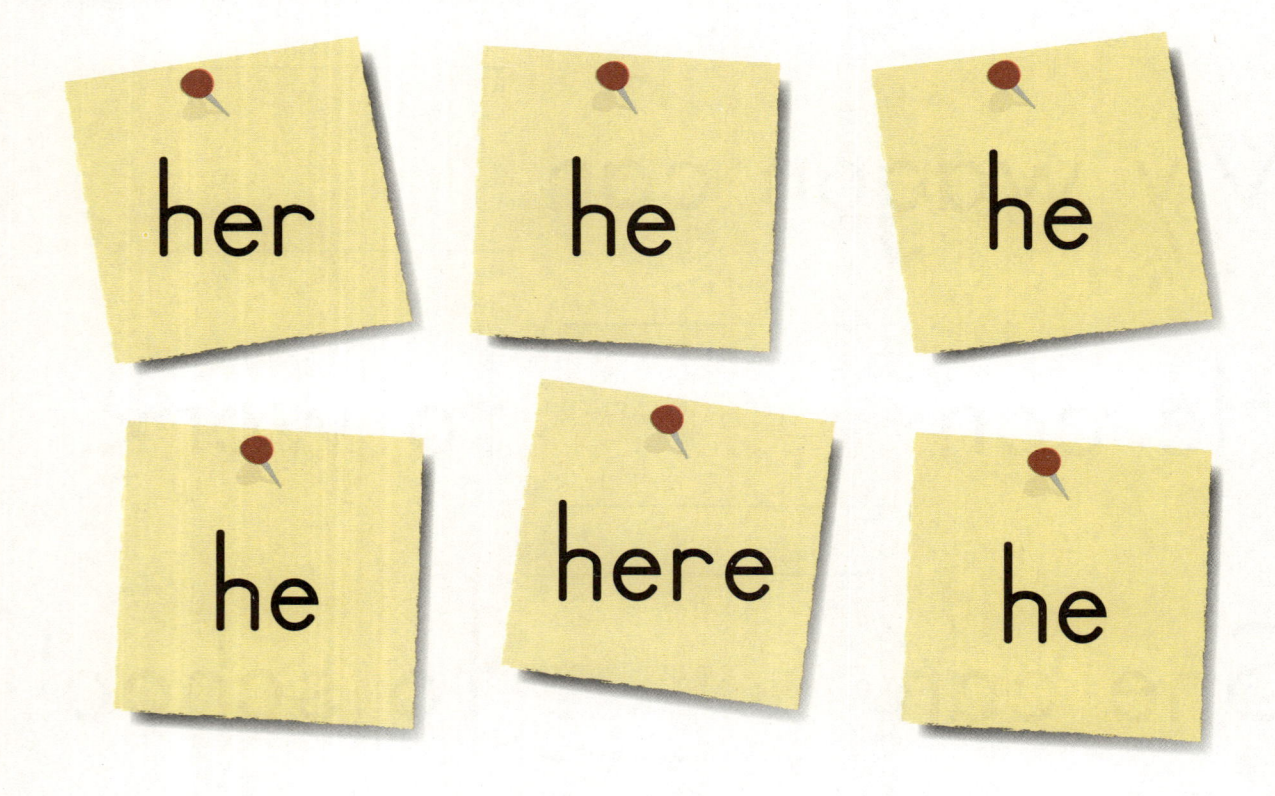

her   he   he

he   here   he

Color the picture whose name begins with the sound you hear at the beginning of **boy**.

Let's Practice Sight Words

Sight Word: her

her

Write the missing letters to spell **her**.

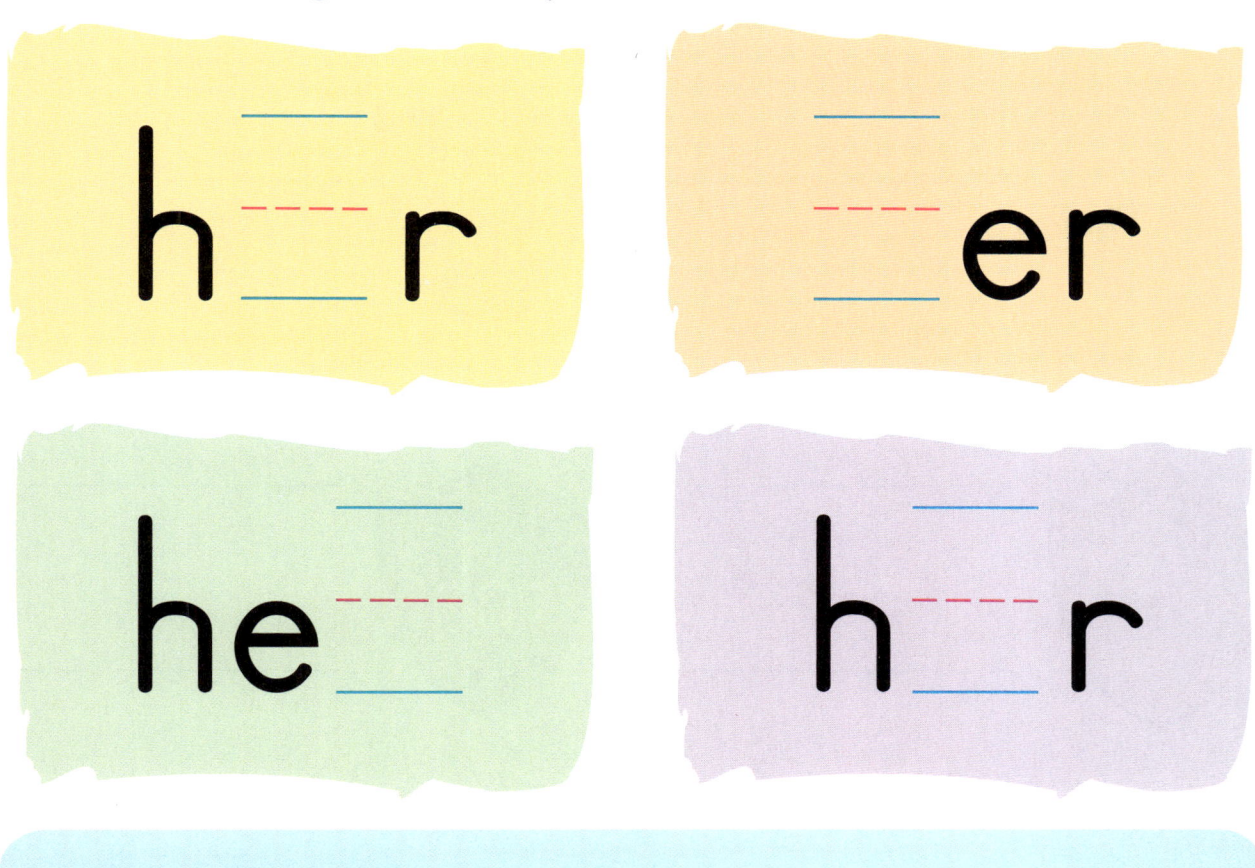

h __ r

__ er

he __

h __ r

Circle the balls with **r**.

h   r   n   r

Let's Practice **Sight Words**

Sight Word: him

him

Unscramble the letters to spell **him**.

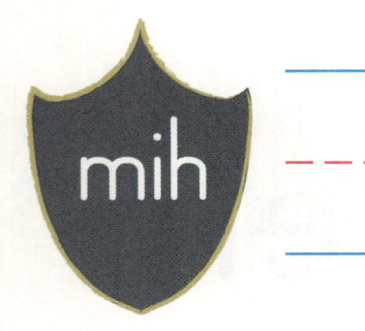

mih

imh

hmi

mhi

Circle the crowns that are the same.

Sight Word: I

I

Write **I** to complete each sentence.

_____ like my pets.

_____ have three dogs.

My dogs and _____ play.

Read the words. Find two pairs of opposites.

awake   old   asleep   new

Let's Practice Sight Words

Sight Word: in

in

Circle **in**. Draw a line to see if you won tic-tac-toe!

it	is	is
is	win	a
in	in	in

Read the color words. Color the socks.

red    green 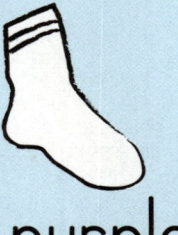   purple    blue

Let's Practice Sight Words

Sight Word: is

is

Write **is** to complete each sentence.

She _____ on the case.

Olivia _____ hungry.

Jose _____ happy.

Trace the path with a crayon three times. Use a different color each time.

Let's Practice Sight Words

Sight Word: it

it

Circle **it**. Draw a line to see if you won tic-tac-toe!

if	in	in
it	it	it
if	is	is

Color the pictures whose names begin with the sound you hear at the beginning of **lion**.

Sight Word: look

look

Write the missing letters to spell **look**.

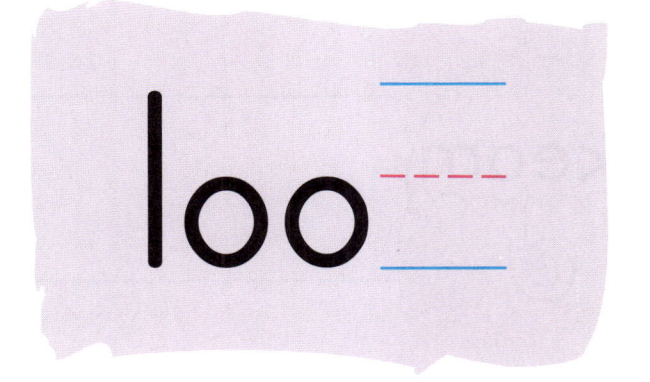

l __ ok

__ ook

lo __ k

loo __

Circle the pictures that go together.

19

Let's Practice Sight Words

Sight Word: make

make

Unscramble the letters to spell **make**.

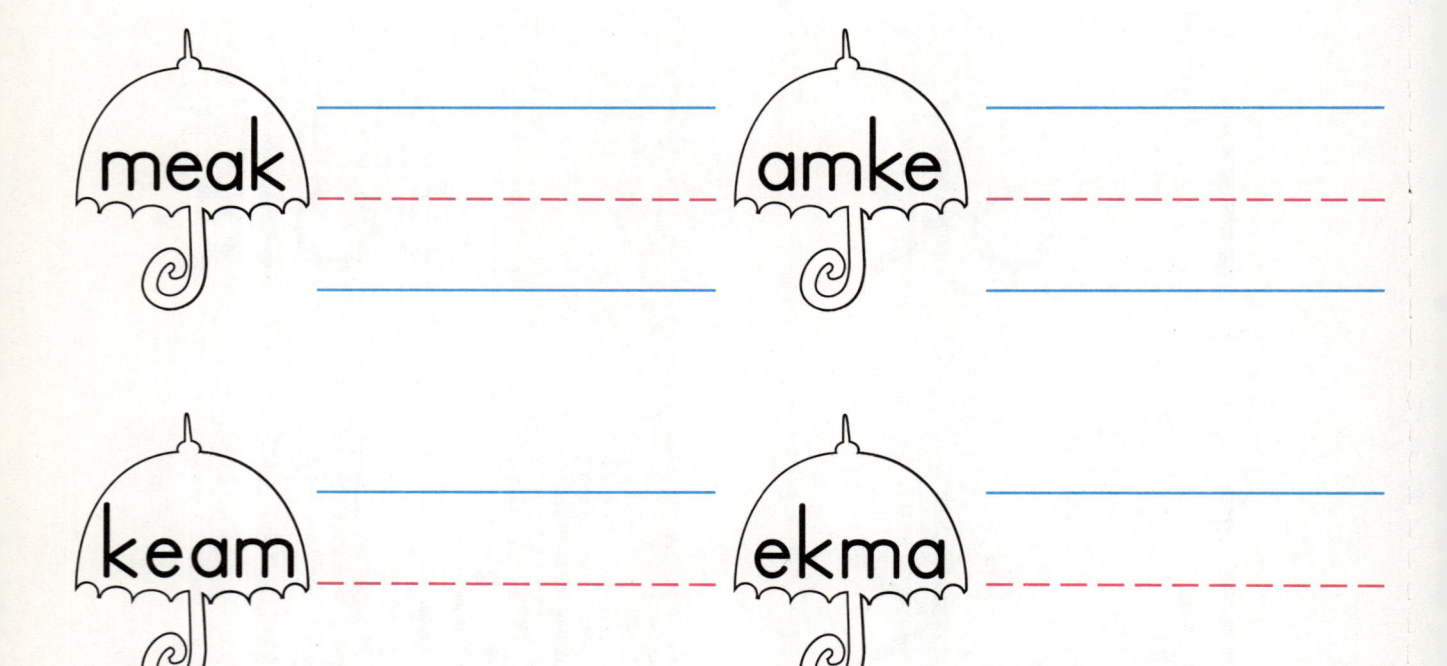

meak _____

amke _____

keam _____

ekma _____

Read the words. Find two pairs of opposites.

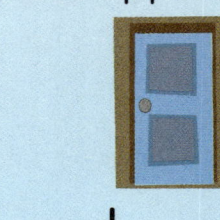

open   full   closed   empty

Sight Word: my

my

Circle the pillows with **my**.

my   my   me

my   ma   my

Trace the path with a crayon three times. Use a different color each time.

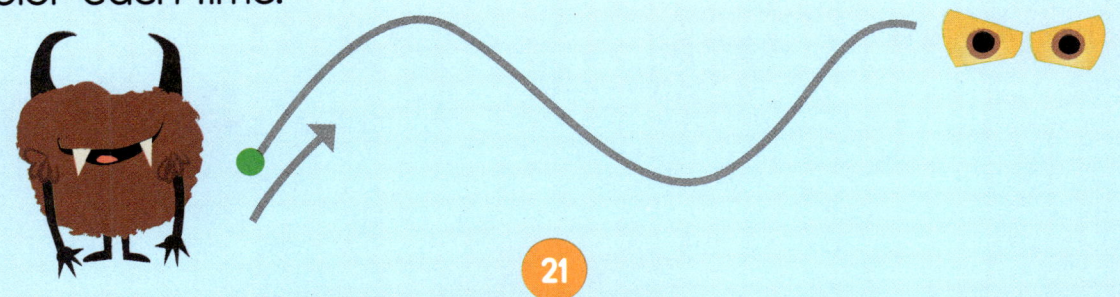

Let's Practice Sight Words

Sight Word: not

not

Write **not** to complete each sentence.

It is ------- open.

I am ------- awake.

She is ------- coming.

In each pair, circle the one that is full.

Sight Word: said

said

Unscramble the letters to spell **said**.

dais

isad

Circle **s** in each word.

sun    snake    bus

23

Let's Practice Sight Words

Sight Word: see

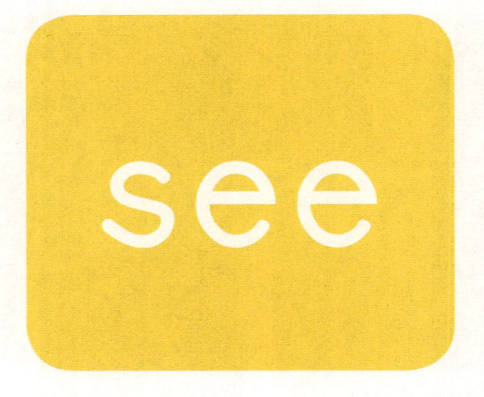

see

Circle **see**. Draw a line to see if you won tic-tac-toe!

seen	see	say
is	see	can
eyes	see	set

Say the name of each picture. Circle the letter that makes its beginning sound.

cat   fork   table

Let's Practice Sight Words

Sight Word: there

there

Write the missing letters to spell **there**.

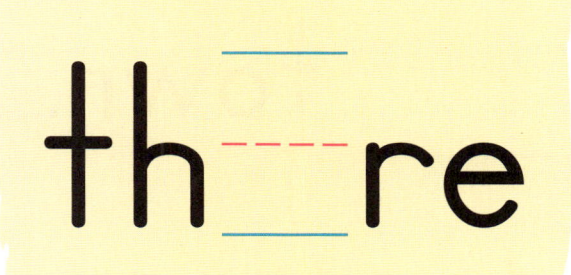

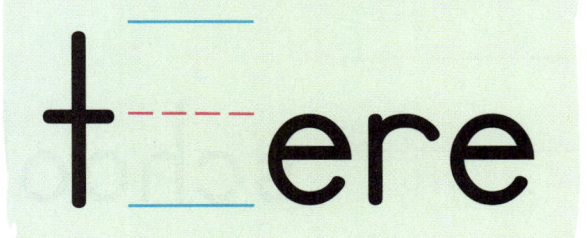

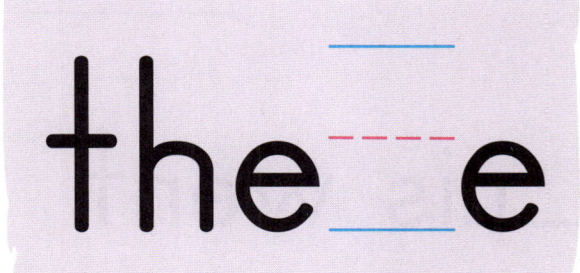

th__re   __here

t__ere   the__e

Color the pictures whose names begin with the sound of **h**.

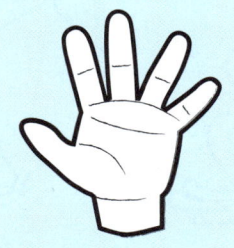

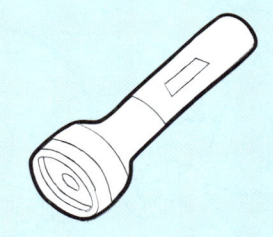

Let's Practice Sight Words

Sight Word: to

to

Write **to** to complete each sentence.

Trains go _____ town.

I have _____ go home.

Luis went _____ school.

Color the toys yellow. Color the animals green.

Sight Word: up

up

Color the planes with **up**.

put
up
up
pup
us
up

Color the cloud with **p**.

b   d   p   o

Let's Practice Sight Words

Sight Word: we

we

Circle **we**. Draw a line to see if you won tic-tac-toe!

we	we	we
was	up	were
to	he	my

Color the shirts that show rhyming words.

clock   lock   can